Lights, camera, fraction!

This CGP book has been carefully crafted to help Year 3 pupils build up all the Fractions skills they need.

It's packed with quick-fire 10-Minute Tests that become more challenging as pupils work through — helping them get used to answering even the toughest questions.

We've even included full answers to every question — plus a handy chart to check progress too!

What CGP is all about

Our sole aim here at CGP is to produce the highest quality books — carefully written, immaculately presented and dangerously close to being funny.

Then we work our socks off to get them out to you — at the cheapest possible prices.

Published by CGP

Editors: Martha Bozic, Liam Dyer, Samuel Mann and Caroline Purvis

With thanks to Gareth Mitchell and Rosa Roberts for the proofreading.

With thanks to Jan Greenway for the copyright research.

ISBN: 978 1 78908 637 9

Clipart from Corel®
Printed by Elanders Ltd, Newcastle upon Tyne.

Based on the classic CGP style created by Richard Parsons.

Text, design, layout and original illustrations © Coordination Group Publications Ltd. (CGP) 2020
All rights reserved.

Photocopying this book is not permitted, even if you have a CLA licence.
Extra copies are available from CGP with next day delivery • 0800 1712 712 • www.cgpbooks.co.uk

Contents

Test 1 2
Test 2 4
Test 3 6
Test 4 8
Test 5 10
Test 6 12
Test 7 14
Test 8 16
Test 9 18
Test 10 20
Test 11 22
Test 12 24
Answers 26
Progress Chart 30

How to Use this Book

- This book contains <u>12 tests</u>, all geared towards improving your fractions skills.

- Each test is out of <u>9 marks</u> and should take about <u>10 minutes</u> to complete.

- Each test starts with some <u>warm-up questions</u> to get you going and ends with a <u>problem-solving question</u>.

- The tests <u>increase in difficulty</u> as you go through the book.

- <u>Answers</u> and a <u>Progress Chart</u> can be found at the <u>back</u> of the book.

Test 1

Warm up

1. Look at these triangles.

   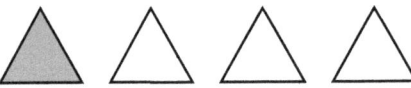

   What fraction of the triangles are shaded?
   Circle the correct fraction.

   $\frac{3}{4}$ $\frac{2}{4}$ $\frac{1}{4}$

   1 mark

2. Shade in $\frac{1}{2}$ of each shape.

   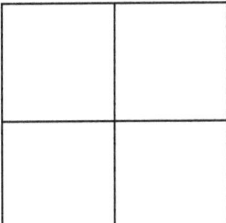   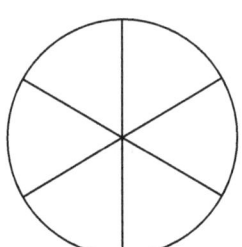

   2 marks

3. Use the pictures to help you work out:

   $\frac{1}{2}$ of 10 = ...

   1 mark

   $\frac{1}{3}$ of 15 = ...

   1 mark

4. Draw lines to match each shape to the correct fraction that is shaded.

   One has been done for you.

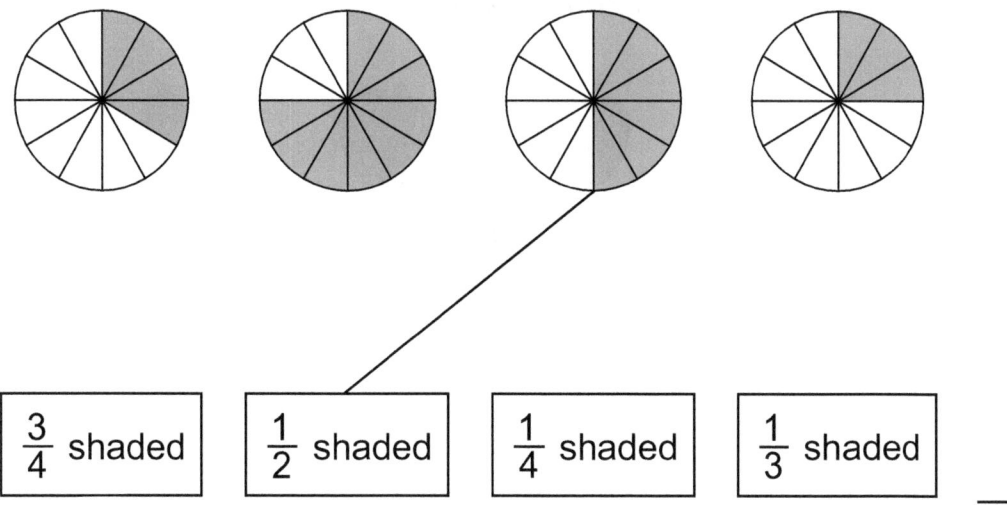

2 marks

5. Kian has a red pencil and a blue pencil.
   The red pencil is 16 cm long. The blue pencil is
   1 cm shorter than half the length of the red pencil.

   How long is the blue pencil?

   ………. cm

   2 marks

END OF TEST

/ 9

Test 2

Warm up

1. Circle one third of the apples shown.

   _____
   1 mark

2. Work out:

   a) $\frac{1}{4}$ of 4 = ...   b) $\frac{1}{2}$ of 12 = ...

   _____
   2 marks

3. Tick the correct box next to the sentence.

   "$\frac{2}{4}$ is the same as $\frac{1}{2}$."   True ☐   False ☐

   _____
   1 mark

4. Elliot puts water in a vase.
   His vase is **more** than half full.

   Which vase below could be his?
   Circle the correct option.

   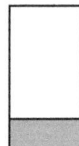   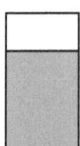   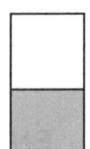

   _____
   1 mark

5. Look at these shapes.

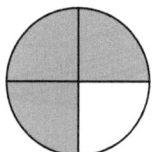 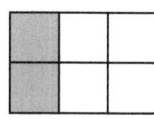 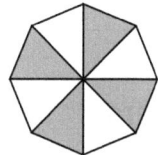 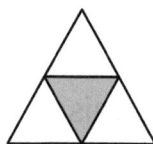

Circle the shape that has exactly $\frac{1}{4}$ shaded.

1 mark

Cross out the shape that has exactly $\frac{1}{2}$ shaded.

1 mark

6. Daisy buys an 8 kg bag of food for her two rabbits. In one month:

- Patches eats $\frac{1}{4}$ of the food.

- Sherbert eats $\frac{1}{2}$ of the food.

How much rabbit food do they eat in total?

.... kg

2 marks

END OF TEST

/ 9

Test 3

Warm up

1. Fill in the missing numbers.

   a) $\frac{1}{4}$ of 12 is ....   b) $\frac{1}{2}$ of .... is 3

   2 marks

2. Circle the smallest fraction below. Use the pictures to help you.

   $\frac{1}{4}$ $\frac{1}{2}$ $\frac{1}{3}$

   1 mark

3. Shade in $\frac{3}{4}$ of this shape.

   1 mark

   Use your answer to find $\frac{3}{4}$ of 20.

   ....   *1 mark*

4. Seren cuts a piece of wood into three equal pieces. She uses two of the pieces to fix a broken chair.

   Circle the fraction of the wood that she has left.

   one third   one quarter   one half

   1 mark

5. Look at the shape below.

   Tick the fraction of the shape that is shaded.

   one half ☐   two quarters ☐

   one sixth ☐   one twelfth ☐

   1 mark

6. Aiza makes a patchwork quilt.
   She uses 15 equal-size pieces of fabric.

   $\frac{1}{5}$ of the quilt is purple and the same fraction is orange.

   How many pieces are **neither** purple or orange?

   .... pieces

   2 marks

   END OF TEST

   / 9

Test 4

Warm up

1. What fraction of these stars are shaded?

 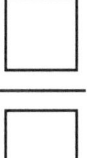

1 mark

2. Shade in $\frac{5}{8}$ of this shape.

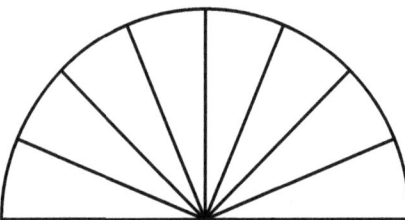

1 mark

3. Draw lines to match each shape to the fraction of it that is shaded.

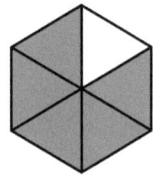 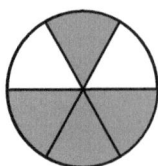 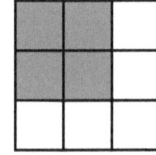 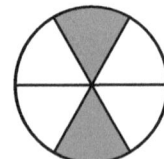

$\frac{2}{3}$ $\frac{5}{6}$ $\frac{1}{3}$ $\frac{4}{9}$

2 marks

4. Fill in the boxes to make each sentence true.

   6 is $\frac{1}{\boxed{}}$ of 18   11 is $\frac{1}{\boxed{}}$ of 22

   2 marks

5. Circle $\frac{2}{3}$ of these marbles.

         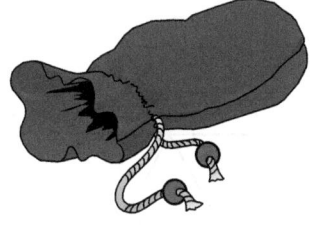

   1 mark

6. Anthony has 14 flowers.
   Cleo has $\frac{1}{2}$ as many flowers as Anthony.

   How many flowers do they have altogether?

   .... flowers

   2 marks

   END OF TEST

   / 9

Test 5

Warm up

1. Circle the correct word to complete the sentence.

    One half is (**bigger** / **smaller**) than one third.

    _____
    1 mark

2. Circle the hexagon that has **less than** $\frac{1}{3}$ shaded.

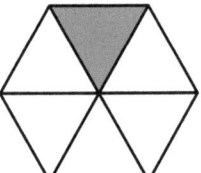 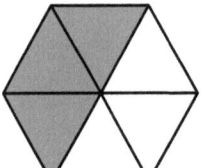 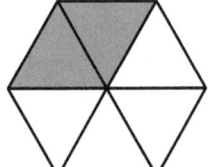 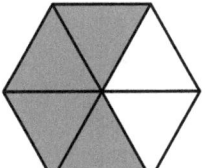

_____
1 mark

3. Write these fractions in the correct place on the number line below.

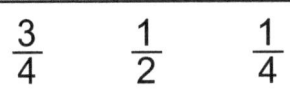

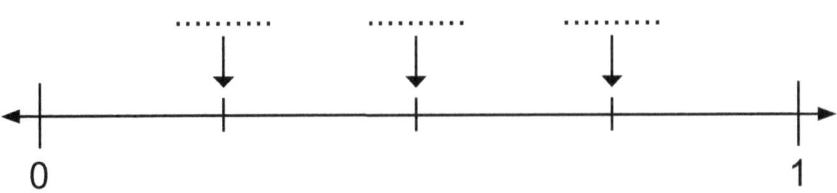

_____
1 mark

4. Shade the second and third shapes so they have the same fraction shaded as the first shape.

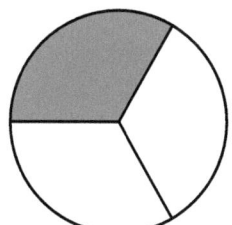 = 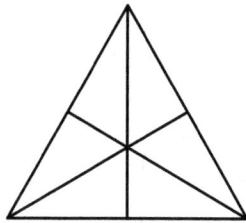 =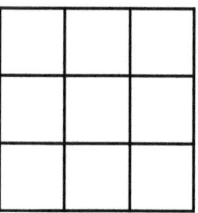

2 marks

5. Work out:

$\frac{1}{4}$ of 36 = ... $\frac{1}{8}$ of 24 = ...

2 marks

6. A pizza is cut into 10 equal slices.
Duncan eats $\frac{1}{5}$ of the slices. Rosa eats 4 slices.
Malcolm eats the rest of the pizza.

How many slices did Malcolm eat?

.... slices

2 marks

END OF TEST

/ 9

Test 6

Warm up

1. What fraction of these acorns are shaded?

   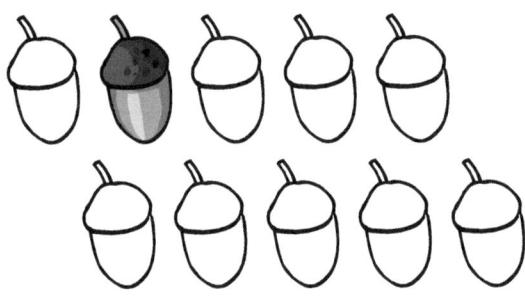 

   1 mark

2. Write a fraction in the gap to make each sentence true.

   a) .... of 9 is 3   b) .... of 20 is 4

   2 marks

3. Shade in four fifths of each of these shapes.

   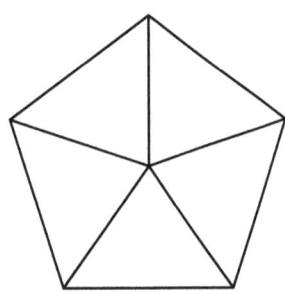 

   2 marks

4. How many **more** of these spaceships need to be shaded so that $\frac{2}{3}$ are shaded in total?

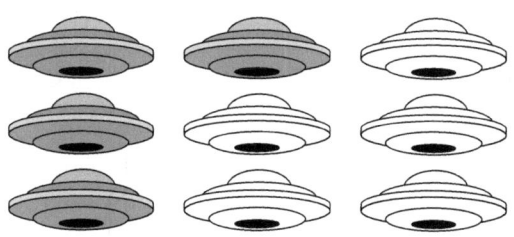

.... spaceships

1 mark

5. Write **<** or **>** in the box to make each statement true.

$\frac{2}{7}$ ☐ $\frac{3}{7}$ $\frac{1}{3}$ ☐ $\frac{1}{4}$

1 mark

6. Priya has 6 toy cars and Talat has 10 toy cars. Priya has 3 blue cars. The same fraction of Priya's and Talat's toy cars are blue.

How many of Talat's toy cars are blue?

.... toy cars

2 marks

END OF TEST

/ 9

 # Test 7

Warm up

1. Circle the jug below that is $\frac{3}{4}$ full.

   _____
   1 mark

2. Circle the smaller fraction in each of these pairs.

   $\frac{2}{3}$ or $\frac{1}{3}$ $\frac{5}{6}$ or $\frac{1}{6}$ $\frac{1}{5}$ or $\frac{2}{5}$

   _____
   2 marks

3. Count up in steps of $\frac{1}{10}$ to fill in the gaps.

   $\frac{1}{10}$ .... $\frac{4}{10}$ .... $\frac{6}{10}$

   _____
   1 mark

4. Circle the fraction below that is equivalent to $\frac{1}{3}$.

   Use the shape on the right to help you.

   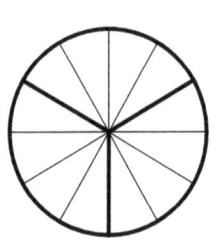

   $\frac{3}{12}$ $\frac{3}{6}$ $\frac{4}{12}$ $\frac{4}{6}$

   _____
   1 mark

5. Work out:

$\frac{2}{3}$ of 24

.... $\overline{\text{1 mark}}$

$\frac{3}{4}$ of 24

.... $\overline{\text{1 mark}}$

6. On Monday, $\frac{1}{2}$ of Cariad's class wore grey trousers. $\frac{1}{3}$ of the class wore black trousers and the rest of the class wore skirts.

There are 18 pupils in Cariad's class.

How many pupils wore trousers on Monday?

.... pupils $\overline{\text{2 marks}}$

END OF TEST

/ 9

Test 8

Warm up

1. Circle the fractions below that are smaller than $\frac{1}{4}$.

   $\frac{1}{2}$ $\frac{1}{5}$ $\frac{1}{3}$ $\frac{1}{10}$

   2 marks

2. Work out these calculations, giving your answer as a fraction:

   a) $1 \div 10 =$ ....   b) $9 \div 10 =$ ....

   2 marks

3. Complete the fractions shown on this number line.

   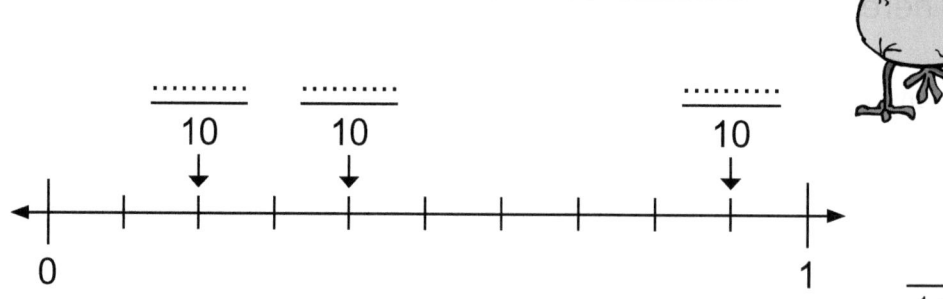

   1 mark

4. Fill in the gaps with the fractions from the box in order from smallest to largest.

   $\boxed{\frac{7}{8} \quad \frac{3}{8} \quad \frac{4}{8}}$

   .... $\frac{5}{8}$ ....

   1 mark

5. Draw two more shapes so that half of the shapes are triangles.

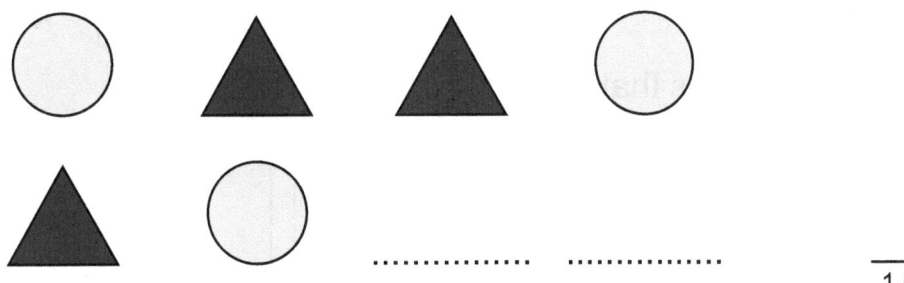

....

1 mark

6. A supermarket sells three sizes of egg boxes, as shown in the table below.

Box size	Number of eggs
Small	? eggs
Medium	12 eggs
Large	30 eggs

A small box has $\frac{1}{5}$ as many eggs as a large box.

How many **more** eggs are there in a large box than in a small box?

.... eggs

2 marks

END OF TEST

/ 9

Test 9

Warm up

1. Tick the shapes that are $\frac{5}{6}$ shaded.

   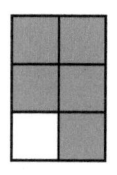 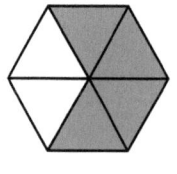 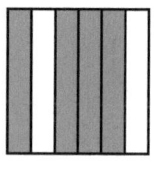 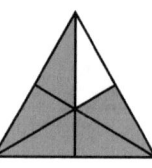

   ☐   ☐   ☐   ☐

   _____
   1 mark

2. Shade in $\frac{3}{4}$ of each of these shapes.

   _____
   2 marks

3. Circle the bigger fraction in each box.

   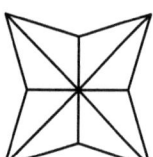   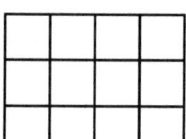

   _____
   2 marks

4. What is $\frac{3}{5}$ of 25?

   .... _____
   1 mark

5. Use the diagram to work out this calculation.

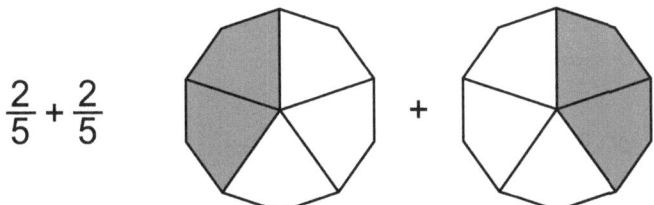

$\frac{2}{5} + \frac{2}{5}$

....
1 mark

6. Jason and Ellie have 40 papers to deliver in total.

   Ellie delivers 21 papers.

   Jason delivers $\frac{1}{3}$ as many papers as Ellie.

   How many papers do they still need to deliver?

.... papers
2 marks

END OF TEST

/ 9

Test 10

Warm up

1. Write these fractions in order from largest to smallest.

    $\frac{1}{12}$ $\qquad$ $\frac{3}{12}$ $\qquad$ $\frac{11}{12}$ $\qquad$ $\frac{7}{12}$

    ....

    1 mark

2. Circle the bigger fraction in each of these pairs.

    $\frac{1}{3}$ or $\frac{1}{5}$ $\qquad$ $\frac{1}{10}$ or $\frac{1}{2}$ $\qquad$ $\frac{1}{7}$ or $\frac{1}{14}$

    2 marks

3. What is 2 tenths more than $\frac{7}{10}$?

    .... 1 mark

    What is 6 tenths less than $\frac{7}{10}$?

    .... 1 mark

4. Use the diagram to work out this calculation.

$\frac{2}{8} + \frac{5}{8}$ 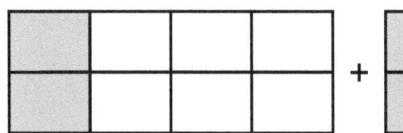 +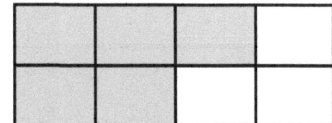

.... ――――
1 mark

5. Circle the shape below that does **not** have the same fraction shaded as the others.

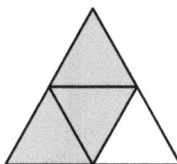 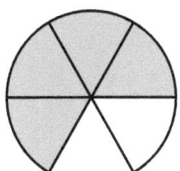 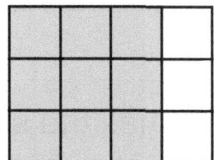 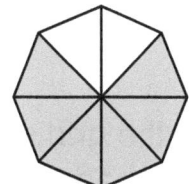

――――
1 mark

6. Miss Salib asked the 24 pupils in her class what their favourite animal is.

$\frac{1}{2}$ of the pupils chose cats. $\frac{1}{4}$ of the pupils chose dogs.

How many pupils did **not** choose either cats or dogs?

.... pupils ――――
2 marks

END OF TEST

/ 9

Test 11

Warm up

1. Count down in tenths from $\frac{6}{10}$.

   $\frac{6}{10}$ .... $\frac{2}{10}$

   1 mark

2. Work out $\frac{1}{10}$ of each of these numbers.

   a) 80: ....   b) 120: ....

   1 mark

3. Shade the grid so that it has the same fraction shaded as the pentagon.

   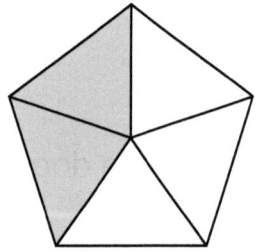 =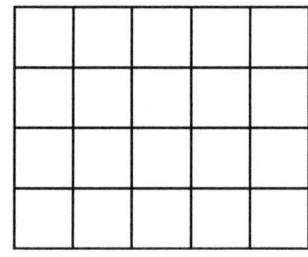

   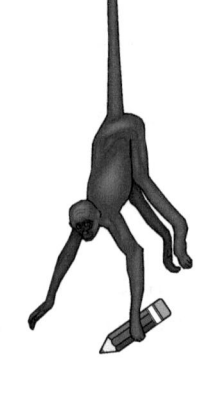

   1 mark

4. Fill in the missing numbers to complete these calculations.

   3 ÷ .... = $\frac{3}{10}$ .... ÷ 10 = $\frac{7}{10}$

   1 mark

5. Write <, > or = in the boxes to make each statement true.

$\frac{1}{2}$ ☐ $\frac{1}{8}$ $\frac{9}{12}$ ☐ $\frac{11}{12}$

2 marks

6. Work out:

$\frac{1}{7} + \frac{2}{7} =$ .... $\frac{4}{5} - \frac{2}{5} =$ ....

$\frac{2}{8} + \frac{3}{8} =$ .... $\frac{9}{10} - \frac{6}{10} =$ ....

2 marks

7. Ian's school bag weighs $\frac{1}{9}$ kg when it is empty. His books weigh $\frac{4}{9}$ kg and his lunch weighs $\frac{3}{9}$ kg.

He puts his books and lunch in his bag.

How much does his bag weigh now?

.... kg

1 mark

END OF TEST

/ 9

Test 12

Warm up

1. Circle the fractions below that are equivalent to $\frac{1}{2}$.

    $\frac{2}{5}$ $\frac{5}{10}$ $\frac{3}{6}$ $\frac{1}{20}$

    1 mark

2. Work out:

   a) $\frac{1}{6}$ of 18 = ...   b) $\frac{1}{5}$ of 25 = ...

   c) $\frac{2}{3}$ of 12 = ...   d) $\frac{3}{4}$ of 20 = ...

   2 marks

3. The circle below is split into 10 equal parts.

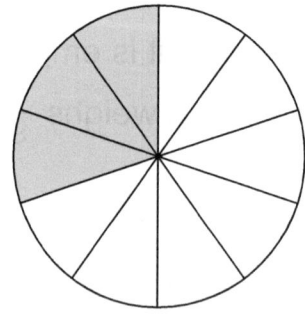

   How many **more** parts need to be shaded so that $\frac{8}{10}$ of the circle is shaded?

   .... parts

   1 mark

4. Write these fractions in order from smallest to largest.

$\frac{1}{9}$ $\frac{1}{3}$ $\frac{1}{15}$ $\frac{1}{6}$ $\frac{1}{12}$

....

1 mark

5. Fill in the missing fractions in these calculations.

$\frac{3}{4} - \ldots = \frac{2}{4}$ $\ldots + \frac{3}{7} = \frac{5}{7}$

$\frac{1}{9} + \ldots = \frac{8}{9}$ $\ldots - \frac{7}{10} = 0$

2 marks

6. Imani has $\frac{10}{11}$ of a whole cake in the fridge.

Her brother eats $\frac{4}{11}$ of the whole cake.

Her sister eats $\frac{3}{11}$ of the whole cake.

What fraction of the cake does Imani have left?

.... 2 marks

END OF TEST

/ 9

Answers

Test 1 – pages 2-3

1. $\frac{1}{4}$ should be circled. (**1 mark**)

2. E.g.  (**1 mark**) (**1 mark**)

3. $\frac{1}{2}$ of 10 = 10 ÷ 2 = 5 (**1 mark**)

   $\frac{1}{3}$ of 15 = 15 ÷ 3 = 5 (**1 mark**)

4.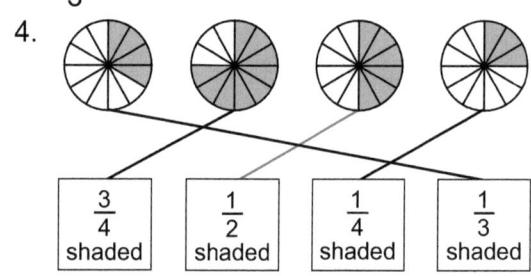

   (**2 marks for all three lines correct, otherwise 1 mark for one correct**)

5. $\frac{1}{2}$ of 16 cm = 16 ÷ 2 = 8 cm.

   The blue pencil is 1 cm shorter, so it is 8 cm – 1 cm = 7 cm long.

   (**2 marks for the correct answer, otherwise 1 mark for a correct method**)

Test 2 – pages 4-5

1. E.g.

   (**1 mark for three apples circled**)

2. a) $\frac{1}{4}$ of 4 = 4 ÷ 4 = 1 (**1 mark**)

   b) $\frac{1}{2}$ of 12 = 12 ÷ 2 = 6 (**1 mark**)

3. True (**1 mark**)

4. 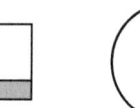   (**1 mark**)

5.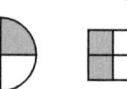

   (**1 mark for the correct shape circled and 1 mark for the correct shape crossed out**)

6. Patches eats $\frac{1}{4}$ of 8 kg = 8 ÷ 4 = 2 kg

   Sherbert eats $\frac{1}{2}$ of 8 kg = 8 ÷ 2 = 4 kg

   So they eat 2 kg + 4 kg = 6 kg of rabbit food in total.

   (**2 marks for the correct answer, otherwise 1 mark for a correct method**)

Test 3 – pages 6-7

1. a) 3 (**1 mark**)   b) 6 (**1 mark**)

2. $\frac{1}{4}$ of 12 = 3, $\frac{1}{2}$ of 12 = 6, $\frac{1}{3}$ of 12 = 4

   So $\frac{1}{4}$ should be circled. (**1 mark**)

3. E.g. 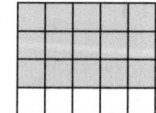 (**1 mark for the correct amount shaded**)

   15 out of 20 squares are shaded, so $\frac{3}{4}$ of 20 = 15. (**1 mark**)

4. She uses two out of three pieces, so there is one piece of wood left. So 'one third' should be circled. (**1 mark**)

5. $\frac{2}{12}$ of the shape is shaded, which is equivalent to $\frac{1}{6}$.

   So 'one sixth' should be ticked. (**1 mark**)

Answers

6. $\frac{1}{5}$ of 15 = 15 ÷ 5 = 3, so there are 3 purple pieces and 3 orange pieces. 15 − 3 − 3 = 9, so 9 pieces are neither purple or orange.
   (**2 marks for the correct answer, otherwise 1 mark for a correct method**)

Test 4 – pages 8-9

1. $\frac{3}{5}$ (**1 mark**)
2. E.g. (**1 mark**)
3. (**2 marks for all four lines drawn correctly, otherwise 1 mark for at least two correct lines**)
4. 6 is $\frac{1}{3}$ of 18   11 is $\frac{1}{2}$ of 22
   (**1 mark for each correct answer**)
5. E.g. (**1 mark for eight marbles circled**)
6. Cleo has $\frac{1}{2}$ of 14 flowers, which is 14 ÷ 2 = 7 flowers. So Cleo and Anthony have 14 + 7 = 21 flowers altogether.
   (**2 marks for the correct answer, otherwise 1 mark for a correct method**)

Test 5 – pages 10-11

1. bigger (**1 mark**)
2. should be circled. (**1 mark**)

3.
   (**1 mark for all three fractions in the correct places**)
4. E.g.
   (**1 mark for each correctly shaded shape**)
5. $\frac{1}{4}$ of 36 = 9 $\frac{1}{8}$ of 24 = 3
   (**1 mark for each correct answer**)
6. Duncan eats $\frac{1}{5}$ of 10 slices, which is 10 ÷ 5 = 2 slices. Duncan and Rosa eat 2 + 4 = 6 slices in total, so Malcolm eats 10 − 6 = 4 slices.
   (**2 marks for the correct answer, otherwise 1 mark for a correct method**)

Test 6 – pages 12-13

1. $\frac{1}{10}$ (**1 mark**)
2. a) $\frac{1}{3}$ (**1 mark**)   b) $\frac{1}{5}$ (**1 mark**)
3. E.g.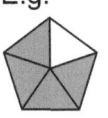
   (**1 mark for each correctly shaded shape**)
4. $\frac{2}{3}$ of 9 spaceships is 6 spaceships. 4 spaceships are already shaded, so 6 − 4 = 2 more need to be shaded.
   (**1 mark**)
5. $\frac{2}{7} < \frac{3}{7}$ $\frac{1}{3} > \frac{1}{4}$
   (**1 mark for both correct**)
6. 3 is $\frac{1}{2}$ of 6, so $\frac{1}{2}$ of Priya's toy cars are blue. $\frac{1}{2}$ of Talat's toy cars are also blue, so $\frac{1}{2}$ of 10 = 5 of Talat's toy cars are blue.
   (**2 marks for the correct answer, otherwise 1 mark for a correct method**)

Test 7 – pages 14-15

1.     (**1 mark**)

2. $\frac{1}{3}$, $\frac{1}{6}$ and $\frac{1}{5}$ should be circled.
   (**2 marks for all three correctly circled, otherwise 1 mark for two correctly circled**)

3. $\frac{1}{10}$, $\frac{2}{10}$, $\frac{3}{10}$, $\frac{4}{10}$, $\frac{5}{10}$, $\frac{6}{10}$ (**1 mark**)

4. $\frac{4}{12}$ should be circled. (**1 mark**)

5. $\frac{1}{3}$ of 24 = 24 ÷ 3 = 8,
   so $\frac{2}{3}$ of 24 = 8 × 2 = 16 (**1 mark**)
   $\frac{1}{4}$ of 24 = 24 ÷ 4 = 6,
   so $\frac{3}{4}$ of 24 = 6 × 3 = 18 (**1 mark**)

6. $\frac{1}{2}$ of 18 = 18 ÷ 2
      = 9 pupils wore grey trousers.
   $\frac{1}{3}$ of 18 = 18 ÷ 3
      = 6 pupils wore black trousers.
   So 9 + 6 = 15 pupils wore trousers.
   (**2 marks for the correct answer, otherwise 1 mark for a correct method**)

Test 8 – pages 16-17

1. $\frac{1}{5}$ and $\frac{1}{10}$ should be circled.
   (**2 marks for both correctly circled, otherwise 1 mark for one correctly circled and no more than one incorrectly circled**)

2. a) $\frac{1}{10}$ (**1 mark**)   b) $\frac{9}{10}$ (**1 mark**)

3.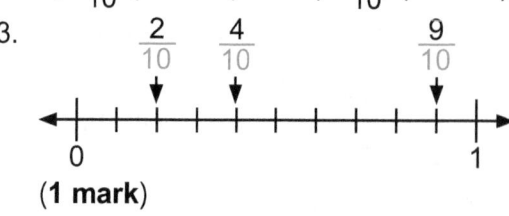
   (**1 mark**)

4. $\frac{3}{8}$, $\frac{4}{8}$, $\frac{5}{8}$, $\frac{7}{8}$ (**1 mark**)

5. There will be 8 shapes, so $\frac{1}{2}$ of 8 = 8 ÷ 2 = 4 shapes must be triangles.
   So draw 1 triangle and 1 other shape.
   E.g.
   (**1 mark**)

6. There are $\frac{1}{5}$ of 30 = 30 ÷ 5 = 6 eggs in a small box. So there are 30 – 6 = 24 more eggs in a large box than in a small box.
   (**2 marks for the correct answer, otherwise 1 mark for a correct method**)

Test 9 – pages 18-19

1.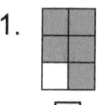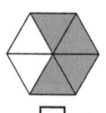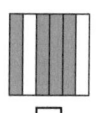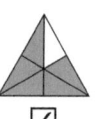
   ☑   ☐   ☐   ☑
   (**1 mark**)

2. E.g.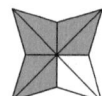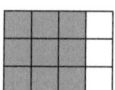
   (**1 mark for each correctly shaded shape**)

3. $\frac{3}{6}$, $\frac{4}{5}$, $\frac{8}{10}$ and $\frac{6}{9}$ should be circled.
   (**2 marks for all four correctly circled, otherwise 1 mark for at least two correctly circled**)

4. $\frac{1}{5}$ of 25 = 25 ÷ 5 = 5,
   so $\frac{3}{5}$ of 25 = 5 × 3 = 15 (**1 mark**)

5. $\frac{2}{5} + \frac{2}{5} = \frac{4}{5}$ (**1 mark**)

6. Jason delivers $\frac{1}{3}$ of 21 = 21 ÷ 3
      = 7 papers
   So they deliver 7 + 21 = 28 papers and have 40 – 28 = 12 papers still to deliver.
   (**2 marks for the correct answer, otherwise 1 mark for a correct method**)

Test 10 – pages 20-21

1. $\frac{11}{12}, \frac{7}{12}, \frac{3}{12}, \frac{1}{12}$ (**1 mark**)

2. $\frac{1}{3}, \frac{1}{2}$ and $\frac{1}{7}$ should be circled.
   (**2 marks for all three correct fractions circled, otherwise 1 mark for at least one correct fraction circled**)

3. Count up 2 tenths from $\frac{7}{10}$:
   $\frac{8}{10}, \frac{9}{10}$ (**1 mark**)
   Count down 6 tenths from $\frac{7}{10}$:
   $\frac{6}{10}, \frac{5}{10}, \frac{4}{10}, \frac{3}{10}, \frac{2}{10}, \frac{1}{10}$ (**1 mark**)

4. $\frac{2}{8} + \frac{5}{8} = \frac{7}{8}$ (**1 mark**)

5. From left to right, the fractions are:
   $\frac{3}{4}, \frac{4}{6}, \frac{9}{12}, \frac{6}{8}$.
   $\frac{3}{4}, \frac{9}{12}$ and $\frac{6}{8}$ are equivalent, so

   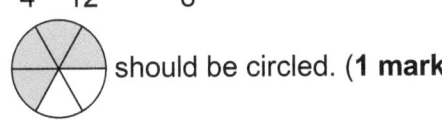 should be circled. (**1 mark**)

6. $\frac{1}{2}$ of 24 = 24 ÷ 2
             = 12 pupils chose cats.
   $\frac{1}{4}$ of 24 = 24 ÷ 4
             = 6 pupils chose dogs.
   So 24 – 12 – 6 = 6 pupils did not choose either cats or dogs.
   (**2 marks for the correct answer, otherwise 1 mark for a correct method**)

Test 11 – pages 22-23

1. $\frac{6}{10}, \frac{5}{10}, \frac{4}{10}, \frac{3}{10}, \frac{2}{10}$ (**1 mark**)

2. a) 8   b) 12
   (**1 mark for both correct answers**)

3. $\frac{2}{5}$ of the pentagon is shaded, so shade in $\frac{2}{5}$ of the grid, e.g.
   (**1 mark for the correct fraction shaded**)

4. $3 \div 10 = \frac{3}{10}$ $7 \div 10 = \frac{7}{10}$
   (**1 mark for both correct answers**)

5. $\frac{1}{2} > \frac{1}{8}$ $\frac{9}{12} < \frac{11}{12}$
   (**1 mark for each correct answer**)

6. $\frac{1}{7} + \frac{2}{7} = \frac{3}{7}$ $\frac{4}{5} - \frac{2}{5} = \frac{2}{5}$
   $\frac{2}{8} + \frac{3}{8} = \frac{5}{8}$ $\frac{9}{10} - \frac{6}{10} = \frac{3}{10}$
   (**2 marks for all four correct answers, otherwise 1 mark for at least two correct answers**)

7. The bag, books and lunch weigh
   $\frac{1}{9}$ kg + $\frac{4}{9}$ kg + $\frac{3}{9}$ kg = $\frac{8}{9}$ kg in total.
   (**1 mark**)

Test 12 – pages 24-25

1. $\frac{5}{10}$ and $\frac{3}{6}$ should be circled. (**1 mark**)

2. a) 3   b) 5   c) 8   d) 15
   (**2 marks for all four correct answers, otherwise 1 mark for at least two correct answers**)

3. 3 parts = $\frac{3}{10}$ of the circle is shaded, so to get 8 parts = $\frac{8}{10}$ shaded, shade in 5 more parts. (**1 mark**)

4. $\frac{1}{15}, \frac{1}{12}, \frac{1}{9}, \frac{1}{6}, \frac{1}{3}$ (**1 mark**)

5. $\frac{3}{4} - \frac{1}{4} = \frac{2}{4}$ $\frac{2}{7} + \frac{3}{7} = \frac{5}{7}$
   $\frac{1}{9} + \frac{7}{9} = \frac{8}{9}$ $\frac{7}{10} - \frac{7}{10} = 0$
   (**2 marks for all four correct answers, otherwise 1 mark for at least two correct answers**)

6. Imani's brother and sister eat
   $\frac{4}{11} + \frac{3}{11} = \frac{7}{11}$ of the cake.
   So Imani has:
   $\frac{10}{11} - \frac{7}{11} = \frac{3}{11}$ of the cake left.
   (**2 marks for the correct answer, otherwise 1 mark for a correct method**)

Progress Chart

That's all the tests in the book done — nice one!

Now fill in this table with all of your scores and see how you got on.

	Score
Test 1	
Test 2	
Test 3	
Test 4	
Test 5	
Test 6	
Test 7	
Test 8	
Test 9	
Test 10	
Test 11	
Test 12	